Public Talk Series : 6

Vedic View and Way of Life

Swami Dayananda Saraswati
Arsha Vidya

Arsha Vidya
Research and Publication Trust
Chennai

Published by :
Arsha Vidya Research
and Publication Trust
32 / 4 ' Sri Nidhi ' Apts III Floor
Sir Desika Road Mylapore
Chennai 600 004 INDIA
Tel : 044 2499 7023
Telefax : 2499 7131
Email : avrandpc@gmail.com

ISBN : 978 - 93 - 80049 - 00 - 7

First Edition : May 2009 Copies : 2000
1st Reprint : November 2009 Copies : 2000

Design :
Suchi Ebrahim

Printed by :
Sudarsan Graphics
27, Neelakanta Mehta Street
T. Nagar, Chennai 600 017
Email : info@sudarsan.com

Contents

Preface

The Vedic vision of oneness is very much manifest in the Hindu culture throughout Bhārat. Some forms of this culture are also seen in the South East Asian countries. The indigenous culture of North and South America, of Europe, even of the African continent, had great reverence to nature as we have. But a tradition of teaching to unfold the vision of oneness, is a privilege enjoyed only by the Hindus. And the vision percolates through the literature, folklores, folk dances and theatre to the people who have no access to the Vedic wisdom. In these seven talks, at Chennai in 2008, I have tried to explore the profundity of Vedic culture unveiled by generations of elders to the people in the hills and forests of Bhārat.

Swami Dayananda Saraswati

Coimbatore
27 April 2009

Key to Transliteration and Pronunciation of Sanskrit Letters

Sanskrit is a highly phonetic language and hence accuracy in articulation of the letters is important. For those unfamiliar with the *Devanāgari* script, the international transliteration is a guide to the proper pronunciation of Sanskrit letters.

अ	*a*	*(but)*
आ	*ā*	*(father)*
इ	*i*	*(it)*
ई	*ī*	*(beat)*
उ	*u*	*(full)*
ऊ	*ū*	*(pool)*
ऋ	*ṛ*	*(rhythm)*
ॠ	*ṝ*	*(marine)*
लॄ	*ḷ*	*(revelry)*
ए	*e*	*(play)*
ऐ	*ai*	*(aisle)*
ओ	*o*	*(go)*
औ	*au*	*(loud)*
क	*ka*	*(seek)* 1
ख	*kha*	*(blockhead)**1
ग	*ga*	*(get)* 1
घ	*gha*	*(log hut)**1
ङ	*ṅa*	*(sing)* 1
च	*ca*	*(chunk)* 2
छ	*cha*	*(catch him)**2
ज	*ja*	*(jump)* 2
झ	*jha*	*(hedgehog)**2
ञ	*ña*	*(bunch)* 2
ट	*ṭa*	*(true)**3
ठ	*ṭha*	*(anthill)**3
ड	*ḍa*	*(drum)**3
ढ	*ḍha*	*(godhead)**3
ण	*ṇa*	*(under)**3
त	*ta*	*(path)**4
थ	*tha*	*(thunder)**4
द	*da*	*(that)**4
ध	*dha*	*(breathe)**4
न	*na*	*(nut)**4
प	*pa*	*(put)* 5
फ	*pha*	*(loophole)**5
ब	*ba*	*(bin)* 5
भ	*bha*	*(abhor)**5
म	*ma*	*(much)* 5
य	*ya*	*(loyal)*
र	*ra*	*(red)*
ल	*la*	*(luck)*
व	*va*	*(vase)*
श	*śa*	*(sure)*
ष	*ṣa*	*(shun)*
स	*sa*	*(so)*
ह	*ha*	*(hum)*

•	*ṁ*	*anusvāra*	(nasalisation of preceding vowel)
:	*ḥ*	*visarga*	(aspiration of preceding vowel)
*			No exact English equivalents for these letters

1.	Guttural	–	Pronounced from throat
2.	Palatal	–	Pronounced from palate
3.	Lingual	–	Pronounced from cerebrum
4.	Dental	–	Pronounced from teeth
5.	Labial	–	Pronounced from lips

The 5th letter of each of the above class – called nasals – are also pronounced nasally.

Talk 1

'Vṛddha-vyavahāra' holds the Vedic view and way of life

The Veda says, *svādhyāyo'dhyetavyaḥ*, one has to study one's own Veda, but unless one studies the Veda, one will not know of this mandate. The problem is solved by what we know as *vṛddha-vyavahāra*, the value structure and behaviour patterns of the elders in the society and family. They give us the knowledge of what one has to do, what one needs to avoid and also the priorities in life. We imbibe all these from the elders. They themselves might not have studied them in detail, but they have imbibed them from people who knew. This is not an ordinary thing. It is the substance of any culture, especially the Bhāratīya culture, which has its roots in the Veda.

Every form of our daily life is but an expression of this Bhāratīya culture, from our saying *namaste*, to applying *tilaka*, to the pursuit of spiritual knowledge. Everything that we do, may not come from our study of the Veda, because most of us do not study it; it comes from *vṛddha-vyavahāra*.

I have verified this. In the Himalayas, there are people in small villages on the slopes which have been tiered for cultivation. *Sādhu*s who go there from Hyderabad, will introduce themselves as being from Rameshwaram, because that is the only distant place they know. Or they will say, they are from Setu. It is the reason why in our traditional parlance there is an expression, *āsetu-himācala-paryantam*, extending from Setu up to the Himalayas. In that expression you have covered the entire Bhārat.

The people in those mountain slopes and valleys have the same culture. You cannot ask this question: 'Where is Bhagavān?' It is a silly question to ask a Hindu. He will look at you up and down to find out whether you are an Indian. You have to ask in a way that will not stun him, so that you can get an answer. The answer is always, 'Bhagavān is everywhere.' I had tried asking the same question to the tribal people in Anaikatti.[1] We call them tribals; and what are we? It is an unfortunate way of dividing ourselves because they seem to be much more cultured in some areas. If you ask one of them the same question, the answer is, "God is everywhere, everything is God." This is Bhārat. The question is answered in the same way, if the person continues to be a Hindu, of course. It is an important clause we have to add these days. For every Hindu, this is the answer.

That everything is Īśvara, Bhagavān, is a Vedic view. *Īśāvāsyam idaṁ sarvam...* (*Īśāvāsya Upaniṣad* 1.1.). *Sarvaṁ khalvidaṁ brahma...* (*Chāndogya Upaniṣad* 3.14.1). All that is there is God—inside, outside, left, right, below, above, and in all directions; east, west, north, south, and the northeast, northwest, southeast, southwest, all is Bhagavān. It is a statement from the *Muṇḍakopaniṣad* (2.2.12).

This world is viewed by a Bhāratīya as Bhagavān. It is purely a Vedic view. A person from a tribal village or his forefathers, never studied the Veda. But his vision is the vision of the Veda. Before he ploughs the land, he does *pūjā* to the land because he is going to tear apart the earth and he does not want to do any harm. A dancer may not know what the Veda is, but before she starts to perform, she touches the platform on which she is going to dance and asks for pardon. Why? The stage is sacred; that is one thing. And then, she is going to pound the platform with her feet, so she asks, "Please pardon me." Only a person who has the Bhāratīya culture, the vision that Īśvara is everything, can do this. There is nothing that is outside Īśvara. But what we come across is only space, air, time, fire, water, earth, all being elements and elementals. We do not see Īśvara. Therefore some people say, 'Because Īśvara is not seen locally, he must be sitting elsewhere.' Any person who is locally available cannot be Īśvara because such a person is limited in every way. How can this person be Īśvara? Since no single person can be Īśvara, the conclusion is, he is elsewhere.

The *śāstra*, however, tells us, all that is here is Īśvara. The one who confronts the world and the world that is objectified by one's senses and by other means of knowing, is all Īśvara. All that one knows through the means of knowledge known as *śabda pramāṇa*, the Veda, is also Īśvara. What is revealed by the Veda is Īśvara, since the Veda itself is non-separate from Īśvara. It is a huge vision; it is not ordinary. It can be a matter of belief or a matter of knowledge. A belief is a judgement before knowledge. One cannot say, 'I believe that you are sitting here, Swamiji.'

I will ask you, "Why?"

"Because you must be sitting there."

"Why? Don't you see me?"

"Yes, I see you. That is why I believe you are there."

When you see, it is direct knowledge. Let us understand this. When you see me, you have direct knowledge. When you guess, it is indirect knowledge. If you just happened to walk into the hall and do not know who is talking here, then you guess it must be Swami Dayananda; it is a guess, a belief. But the perception that there is one swami sitting here and talking, is not a matter of belief. Therefore, a belief is a judgement before knowledge, and as such, it is subject to correction on verification.

Suppose I say, between Gangotri and Uttarakashi, there is a small village called Gangnani. It has a hot water spring, and next to it there is also a stream of cold water coming down. This is Gangnani. I am choosing this because many of you might not know about Gangnani. Now, since Swamiji has told about it, you assume that it must be there. It is verifiable. You can go to Gangnani and verify what I said, and say, 'Swamiji is right.' What does it mean? It means your belief is subject to verification.

Whatever you understood from my words about Gangnani is indirect knowledge. In fact, it is not even knowledge, but a belief. You take my words as valid, because of *śraddhā*. I became one whose words are trusted to be valid. But it is purely a belief subject to correction on verification. When you go to the Himalayas and see Gangnani, what you see may not match your image born of my words. Even so, you will still know that there is a hot water spring and cold water stream. But knowledge of the whole area of Gangnani, the environment, and the type of mountains that are there, is gained by perception. Therefore, prior to that perception, it is a belief.

The Veda tells you, all that is here is Īśvara. It is the Vedic vision and our culture is based upon this vision. Nobody can gainsay this. This country, Bhārat, is the only land, *puṇya-bhūmi*, in the world where there is the appreciation that everything is Īśvara. Some people have reverence for nature; that is a different thing. All indigenous cultures the world over had held the world in reverence until the new proposition, that the world is created for human consumption, came into vogue. That God created the world for your consumption is an unacceptable concept.

If you extend this, it means you can eat each other because your world consists of human beings too. This propagated concept destroyed the reverence for nature in most of the continents.

Here, we are not talking of just reverence. We are making an equation between you, the subject, and Īśvara who is everything, and the object you confront, a micro object like an electron or a macro object like a flower, a star, the cosmos. Well, this subject-object unit is a whole, and it is Īśvara. The subject is Īśvara, the object is Īśvara. It is something more than mere reverence. If there is reverence, then your reverence also includes you. This is the vision, and it percolates, through *vṛddha-vyavahāra,* to the last man in Cape Comerin and to the people in the Himalayas; it is the same reverence.

It is an equation like energy being matter expressed in the famous equation $E=mc^2$. To understand this equation you have to study. First you need to complete high school, then go to college, where you must study physics. Then, perhaps, you will understand all the implications and the truth of this Einsteinian equation. Many years of study are required just to gain the basic structure to understand what it is all about.

Here, my whole life is committed to understanding this equation—*yadidaṁ sarvam*, all that is here, all that I see, including the seer, is one whole, Īśvara. If this is what is said, then it is not a matter for belief but a matter for knowing. An equation is not to be believed; it is not meant for that. I can have *śraddhā*, pending understanding because in the beginning it will not look possible. 'If everything is Īśvara, why do I not see Īśvara?' What you see is Īśvara. Therefore, you need that trust in order to know, *śraddhāvān labhate jñānam*, the one who has *śraddhā* gains knowledge.[2]

It is a challenge. If a child is told by the elementary school teacher that 6 plus 3 is equal to 100 minus 91, he will blink, wondering, "How is that? On this side there are single digit numbers, 6, 3, and a plus sign. On the other side, a three-digit number, a two-digit number, and a minus sign." Confusion. The boy has to understand it, and the teacher's job is to make him understand. The teacher asks the boy, "Do you understand?" Now suppose the boy says, "I do not understand, Sir, but I believe you!" The teacher is pleased, and tells him, "Sit down." Only if there is *puṇya* will one get a good teacher. With a teacher like that, the boy when he grows up will say, "Swamiji, I am very weak in maths." Nobody is weak in maths. If a child says, 'I am weak in maths,' then that boy or girl should go to a tutor who will help the child go back, and start from the beginning. When the student says, 'I know this,' and proves that he or she knows, then the tutor will keep going. Suddenly the tutor will find there is an area which the student does not know. That is the starting point of all the student's problems, and it is where the tutor begins to help the student understand.

It is the same here. It is an amazing vision which is to be understood. It is the basis of the Vedic view. What objection can one have? The basic vision that is revealed by the Veda is a matter for understanding. A person who follows a given religion needs to ask, 'What is the message? How do I look at myself? And what should I achieve?' At least you ask these questions to whoever preaches religion. One religion preaches, 'You are born of sin, called original sin.' 'What did I do?' 'You have parents, and whoever has parents is born of sin.' Then, I need to be saved. That is the second thing. I must know that this is their view and way of life. And I say, I do not believe it. Then the whole thing falls apart. Please understand this.

According to that religion, in this life I cannot get anywhere because I am imperfect; I am born imperfect and I need to be saved. Only after death will I go to heaven, and I have only one chance here. Their view and way of life is based on the premise that I am imperfect. There are certain other belief systems which are more moderate, but every religion has to tell me what is my goal. And who is 'me'?

Here, I come to the Veda. It tells me, all that is here is Īśvara, including me. I am challenged. I am not asked to believe anything here. Therefore this tradition does not stand opposed to any belief system. It is entirely different.

There was a conference in our Gurukulam in Coimbatore on 'Spirituality and Science' organised by a group which has been conducting this in different places. Quite a few learned people had come to this conference, and they raised the question of spirituality being at loggerheads with science. I had a few minutes to talk to them and told them, "We have no conflict. Science is talking about this world that can be objectified by the subject, the knower. Anything we objectify, whether it is electron, a fact of chemistry, of biochemistry, it is within the purview of science. Its scope is what we can objectify. The Veda does not talk about what we objectify, or what we can objectify. It talks about something that we cannot objectify. Therefore it is not in conflict with science. But what the Veda says has neither an internal contradiction nor is it opposed by any other means of knowledge. It is unopposed. It is *abādhitaṁ jñānam*, knowledge that cannot be negated. It stands true for all time."

The Vedic vision is not ordinary, and the Hindu *dharma* based upon this vision is not one among many religions based on only beliefs. Whatever you confront, including the confronting person, you, the subject, form the whole, and the whole is one Īśvara. And this vision, I find, percolates in every form of Bhāratīya culture. If everything is one whole, you are not part of the whole; you are the whole. What is whole is not made up of parts; it is one whole.

One missionary was to come to India from America and settle down in Tamilnadu, since Tamilnadu had a lot of missionary activities. On his way to India, he thought he would visit and photograph some of the cathedrals in

Southeast Asia. He went to China, and in Peking he visited an old cathedral where he saw one huge golden telephone. He thought it was a toy telephone. He asked the priest there,

"What is this telephone? Is it functional?"

"It is a functional telephone, but it is a special telephone. You can dial God."

"I can dial God, you mean?"

"Yes, Sir."

Then he asked, "What does it cost?"

"10,000 American dollars," said the priest.

"Oh!"

He said, "Where will I go for 10,000 dollars?"

He just moved to other places. He went to Vietnam and found the same type of telephone and their charges were the same; he went to Indonesia and saw a cathedral which also had the telephone. There too, the priest said it cost 10,000 US dollars to make a call.

Then he came to Chennai, India, his ultimate destination. He asked the taxi driver, "Can you take me around before you take me to Santhome cathedral?" The taxi driver took him to some places, and then to the famous Mylapore[3] temple.

The missionary asked, "O! What is this? Is it a Hindu temple?

"Yes, it is a Hindu temple."

"Can I go inside?"

"You can go."

He went inside and he was taking many pictures with admiration. There, again, he saw the same telephone, this golden telephone. It was huge. He asked the priest who was there,

"Is this a telephone?"

"Yes, it is telephone."

"What kind of telephone?"

"You can speak to God."

"I can speak to God?"

"Yes."

"What is the cost?"

"One rupee."

"One rupee? In the catherdrals they said it is 10,000 American dollars."

"Sir, there it is long distance call; here it is a local call, sir," replied the priest touching his heart.

It is local. But still, you have to call. This is exactly what the teaching is about; what these talks are about. You have to make a call.

In our day-to-day life, whatever we do has some connection to religion. We do not see anything that is not connected.

Our tradition is part of this vision; it confirms the vision, gives the stamp, "Yes, this is true; I belong to this Vedic vision." It is confirmed at every stage for every Bhāratīya. The forms are assimilated with that spirit. Then the final launch is taken care of by the very Veda itself, in the form of a dialogue between a teacher and a student.

The teacher-student situation is also integral to the Vedic way of life, which is why you will never find the teaching without the word *uvāca*, he/she said. Even in the *purāṇa*s there is always *uvāca*, he/she said. Some of the *upaniṣad*s may not have the names of the teacher and student involved, but we can see that it is a dialogue like *Kenopaniṣad*. It starts with a question, "*kena iṣitam…, preṣitam…*, willed by whom, impelled by whom?" A student is asking the question, the teacher is answering it. At the end of it one student asks, 'Please teach me *upaniṣad*.' In every *upaniṣad*, we find a dialogue going on because what is involved is a vision that is to be understood. Where nothing is to be understood but something is to be believed, we do not need a dialogue. Wherever there is dialogue, there is assimilation involved because knowledge cannot be fraught with doubts, much less error.

In these few talks to follow, we will unfold the vision and cover a way of life to receive this vision. All that is necessary for this vision, and its significant features, we will cover. We are going to get into the *āraṇya*, forest, of the Veda.

Talk 2

Bridges to the vision of the Veda; The Vedic View of Life

In the *Sāma-veda*, we hear a very beautiful hymn, *setūṁstara. Tara,* cross, using the *setu*. A *setu* can be a bridge, or even a causeway, which is the *upāya*, the means, for crossing what is to be crossed, and is otherwise very difficult to cross, *dustarān setūṁstara.*

"*Dānena adānaṁ tara, akrodhena krodhaṁ tara, śraddhayā aśraddhāṁ tara, satyena anṛtaṁ tara, setūmstīrtvā svar gaccha jyotirgaccha*: overcome the incapacity to give by giving; by refraining from anger, overcome anger; by trust, overcome lack of trust; by truth, overcome what is false; having crossed this four-fold difficult-to-cross human traits, may you gain happiness."

Every individual, by nature, is insecure right from childhood. A human child, being what it is, is helpless, one hundred percent helpless. Any living organism wants to live. It is innate, instinctual. So it always has the fear of death. It is inborn. The urge to live comes along with the fear of death. Naturally, if there is no problem of living, there will be no fear of death. Being a living organism, a child is given the urge to live, but it does not know how to go about. It does not have the capacity, the skills, the wherewithal to survive. Before it was born, it was secure, connected to its *jananī*, the mother. Then the connection was snapped, and it had to start an independent life, a life independent of its mother. What a start! It cannot turn, it cannot walk, much less can it talk, and it is supposed to live an independent life. So the child's helplessness is compensated by the trust it has for the one who cares for it. It does not even know, 'This is my mom.' Perhaps it can vaguely recognise the voice as one that was heard prenatally, but it has no choice. The caring person is trusted totally.

We need to understand this. The child with the help of trust is free from panic. Otherwise it will die from sheer fright. It is free from panic because of total trust in the person who cares for it. And the trust needs to be total because the helplessness is total. The child cannot afford to distrust the person who cares for it. When the trust is total, the trusted person, by implication, is all-knowing, all powerful, all skillful. The child does not know all that, but this is the implication, because the child relaxes itself in the hands of the caring person. It may be the mother or it may be a foster mother, the child has no option. But then, the mother, or anyone else who takes care of the child, is not omniscient, is not omnipotent either. She is a limited human being. She is bound to be inconsistent, to be angry now, loving now; she is bound to fall ill. And the modern mother is bound to send the child, when it is two and a half, to a pre-KG school because she worries, 'What will my child do in this competitive world?' This is how the child gathers all its unconscious core issues. Up to the age of four and a half, the unconscious containing buried issues is formed. After that, the problems are conscious. When the child is less than four, it has got to be with its mother, but it is banished to school. What is it going to think with its innocent mind? In the child's mind, the thought will be, 'I am no good which is why I am banished.' Insecurity increases with every day. Every human being has to go through this childhood, and, therefore, there is every reason to be a 'hood' later. If there are some good *saṁskāras*, the person can escape that.

Insecurity is the very essence of the person's ego, the *ahaṅkāra*. When there is so much insecurity, we cannot be giving and sharing. We can only grab and hold on to it. We can never be big in heart; we are small. We may not be able to give because we may not have the resources to give; that is a reality. But the attempt to give is what matters. If we ask someone to give something for a good cause, the tendency of the other is to think, 'How can I answer this fellow?' We are all very clever people. Somebody asks for a job, and we wonder how to answer him; there is not even sympathy.

A fully mature adult human being is a contributor. If you are a consumer most of the time, and not a contributor, then your life is not in keeping with the Vedic view of life. You have to be a contributor. A child is largely a consumer because the child needs to grow to become an independent adult to contribute. As a parent you can make your child feel that he or she is also a contributor. The parents have to be intelligent for that. When the child does something that is wonderful in its own vision, like getting up on a stool and jumping off, it looks at you as though it has accomplished something big. It is an opportunity for you to make the child feel as a contributor. For you, as an adult, it is nothing; but you can be like a child and appreciate what the child's feeling is, you can look into the eyes of the child and make him feel good, make him understand how he has contributed to your joy. You have already converted a consumer child into a contributor in its very childhood. The child who is appreciated does not feel totally helpless, does not feel, 'I am useless,' which it would otherwise think because the poor child does not know, 'I am also going to walk later, I am going to talk later.' Even if you tell, "You will grow big like us," it can hardly comprehend fully what it takes to be an adult. In the absence of this knowledge the child begins to loath itself.

Self-loathing is a kind of self de-valuation. You can neutralise that feeling to some extent if you, as mother or father, look into the eyes of the child with an overt expression of joy. Because of the child you pick up joy, and you make the child understand that. Then the child will think, 'I am a somebody.'

People do not have this understanding, nor do they have any time. They also have some false ideas about how to raise children. A child goes to school and comes home with marks of 88, 90 and so on. The father's response is all monosyllabic—eh. Or a second response is, 'Uh, not bad, but make your English 100 next time, and Mathematics 100.' The child will feel, 'I cannot win.' But inside, the father is happy. What is wrong if he shows it overtly? The father will say, 'If you tell the child, he will become proud.' Let the child be proud of himself or herself; life will take care of the pride later. Let the child grow with self-pride, self-dignity, self-respect, self-worth and self-esteem; it is all that is required. Life will teach the child that he or she is a limited person. We need not teach.

You have to convert the consumer into a contributor. You are a consumer all the way up to your adulthood. Later you become a contributor also, while the consumer status continues. As you grow up, you consume more and continue to be a consumer, but then, contribute very little. Is that growth? No. In fact, the one who contributes as well, of course consumes, is a grown up person, a mature person. Then, the one who contributes more than he or she consumes, is a much more mature person. The one who consumes the minimum, only enough to maintain the body, and contributes the maximum, is a *mahātmā* in our country, in the Vedic vision. Gandhiji was called a *mahātmā* because he lived with the minimum and contributed his entire life to the public causes for which he was working. He deserved to be called *mahātmā, mahān ātmā yasya,* the one whose mind, *antaḥ-karaṇa,* is big.

How do you become big? In the Vedic vision, you do not become big one fine day. There are people who say, 'Some people are born big, some people are born small.' No. You become big. Sometimes, even without knowing it you become big. Everybody is born small because everybody is born insecure and therefore a consumer. You become a contributor only when you are very secure on your own feet, your emotional feet. It has to be accomplished.

The way of life should be such that it makes you grow into the bigness that you are capable of. Until then, you are small in an adult body, you are not going to be satisfied. There can never be a sense of fulfilment of 'I have made it,' when you are small because there is always fear, and when there is fear you cannot be big. You can have a palatial home because you know it is a solid investment, but then it implies you are insecure. When you have the bigness that I am talking about, it means you are secure. The self-conscious, and, therefore, the self-judging human being has to free himself or herself from this fear that grips the person due to insecurity. 'What will happen? If everything goes away, what will happen? What will happen to my child?' You have to trust in yourself. You think, 'I made it somehow because my father-in-law helped me.' You do not trust that you have made it. If you have self-trust, for which you have to be big, then you need not keep so much for your children. Educate the children; they will take care of themselves and others. It is the duty of the parents to make the children grow to be big, for which the children have to see the father being big and the mother being big. To grow into a big person, and help others grow is our culture, and this growth does not happen without your own initiative.

The *sāma-mantra* tells us, '*dānena adānaṁ tara,* by giving, overcome the incpacity to give.' I am just astounded by this thinking. Modern society in America has a new *mantra,* 'fake it and make it.' To be kind, act kindly. Kindness is a disposition which comes from self-sufficiency. The more adequate you feel about yourself, the kinder you will be towards yourself and others. Even without feeling adequate, you can act kindly. That is what the will is for, the will given to you by Bhagavān.

You are endowed with a free will. There is always a question, 'Swamiji, is there free will or destiny?' There is free will because destiny was earned by free will. Putting it the other way, if there is no free will, you will not have destiny. So destiny is *puṇya-pāpa* earned by a human being who has free will. We can say, free will is the cause for destiny. If destiny brought a body for you wherein free will is possible, it means you have both destiny and free will. The question of free will and destiny is persistent. If I invite questions from the audience, out of 100 questions, 65 will be on destiny and free will! Because some people are convinced that there is no free will, and there are also books that advocate this.

It is free will that makes you different from other beings. Your will can be weak, and if it is, you seek support, seek help from people and form a support group. This is very common in the West. They have various support groups, for obese people, for alcoholics. Then there are groups for the significant people who are around the alcoholics, the co-dependents and they all come together in their own groups. The adult children of alcoholics have problems, and they all join together. Hermits join together. These are people who are shy, who do not socialise, due to reasons locked in the unconscious. They cannot come out and talk to people and live a shell-life. But then, all such people join together and socialise. That is the trick, *upāya*, the *setu* mentioned in the hymn *setūṁstara*.

Dānena adānaṁ tara. Adānam means your incapacity to give, your tendency to grab. Whenever you are introduced to someone you think, 'How can I make use of this introduction?' This particular thinking is vulturous, it is just shallow. But it can be overcome by giving.

How can you be big? Some people think that unless you have money, you cannot be big. Well, if you have money, you can also become smaller. Money does not make you big; you are big. There are many ways of giving. You can give your time, you can lend your ears by listening to someone, good words you can tell, you can pray for somebody. There are so many ways of giving. You become big by doing actions you would do if you were big, by acting as though you are big; *dānena adānaṁ tara.*

Suppose you say, "Unless I have the heart to give, how will I give?" You will get the heart; it will come by giving. How do you learn to cook? Only by cooking. By swimming you learn to swim. Only by driving the car you learn to drive. You cannot put the car in the garage, sit in it and turn the steering wheel for one hour daily in the morning. You do not learn like that. You learn to drive only by driving. So too, by giving you become a giver, *dānena adānaṁ tara.* What a beautiful *vākya*! I am told that the Kanchi senior *ācārya* used to ask any *śrauti*, a *sāma pundit* who went to him to recite this particular hymn, *setūṁstara*. It is obvious he knew the importance of this. By giving, you become a giver, you become big, you become a contributor. Just use the will. Action is the key.

If you act lovingly, you will discover love which is why love is both a noun and verb. You discover love, the noun, by acting lovingly, acting as though you have love. One person told me,

"I hate this person sitting next to me in the office."

"Why?" I asked him.

"Because he got the promotion."

"Why did you not get the promotion?"

"Because I do not have a godfather there; nobody is there to help me."

"Alright, he has somebody to help him and therefore he is qualified."

"He is not qualified, I am qualified."

"Then why did you not get the promotion?"

"Because he has somebody there."

"Well, that is the qualification you must have for promotion. You do not have it; you have everything else."

"Yet I hate him."

"Do you like being a hateful person?"

"No Swamiji, I am a spiritual person."

"Then why do you hate somebody? If somebody is happy, why not be happy? Just looking at that person you can be happy. These are all bits of happiness that you can get easily without any money involved."

"No Swamiji, whenever I look at him my blood pressure goes up."

"Then do one thing. Tell him, 'you know, I hate you. But I do not like this hatred, and I want to get rid of it. I listened to a talk of a Swami. He tells that I should give you one rose daily. Do not mistake me; I am not crazy. I will give you a rose every day for 48 days; please accept it.' "

On the first day he could not even look at the person while giving the rose. On the second day, the angle of his face turns slightly towards the person. On the third day, slightly more; so too on the fourth day, fifth day, sixth day, until on the seventh day, he need not give a rose at all. Why? His hatred is gone. Act it out. This is how *pratipakṣa-bhāvanā* works. Act it out; it will work.

From the morning *kolam*[4] onwards, which is a *bhūta-yajña,* we act. It is our culture. Not only is the *kolam* a symbol of welcoming Lakṣmī, Goddess of Prosperity, it is an art. What a geometry! Without studying geometry, without any device, these women place all these dots with rice powder which they connect to form complex geometric patterns. I used to watch that. When we tried to draw with a compass and all our geometry tools, we could not get anything like that. But they had never gone to school, and yet they made all these complicated, beautiful, amazing designs. They already had the whole map in their mind, brilliant. This is our culture. It is also a *yajña;* the birds and the ants will eat the rice powder. And the one who is drawing the *kolam* must be aware, 'I am doing a *yajña.*' It is a simple act of caring, doing which one becomes a caring person.

Akrodhena krodhaṁ tara. If you are caring, you know how not to get hurt. You can even care for the hurting person, because you do not get hurt. That is the best insulation you can have in yourself. *Akrodhena krodhaṁ tara,* by not being angry, you cross anger. What kind of advice is this? If you are not angry, then you need not cross anger.

Here, you need to act it out. You refrain from acting angrily, and act as though you have no anger, *akrodhena*. Act like that. You do not victimise anybody with your anger, neither your children, nor your spouse, nor anyone else. A spouse is not one on whom you can release all your anger. That is wrong. You have no right to victimise anybody because everybody has the right not to be a victim. It is human dignity; it is a human right—for a male, for a female, for everyone. To help you, the *sāma-mantra* says, *akrodhena krodhaṁ tara*. Just begin. Even if you are angry, practice restraint, *dama*, telling yourself, 'I will not victimise anybody with my anger. I have to release my anger, of course, but I will not vicimise anyone.' How do you release your anger? You can write it out. Process it. You can get angry with Bhagavān; we even have such songs. In one of his songs, Saint Tyagaraja complains to Lord Rāma:

> 'Why are you looking at me like this? You are such a great exalted person in the family of Raghu, why do you look at me from the corner of your eye? What will happen to you if you look at me straight? A Lord of your stature, who are you? Who am I?'

This is one *bhāvanā*. Tyagaraja expressed his anger, everything, through songs. He processed all his emotions through his songs. It was all processing. You also need to process your emotions, and not victimise people. For this processing, we all have songs to sing.

Anger has to be processed, and writing is the best way. You write your anger out. This should be a routine, whenever, of course, there is anger. Without victimising anybody, including yourself, you process the anger by writing it out. Then we have *śama*, but first *dama—akrodhena krodhaṁ tara.*

Śraddhayā aśraddhāṁ tara. If you do not have *śraddhā* in rituals, nor you have *śraddhā* for the elders or for books like the *Gītā* and so on, act as though you have *śraddhā*. Begin doing what you could never do. Act as though you have *śraddhā*, even though there is no *śraddhā*. If you do the same thing that the elders have been doing, *vṛddha-vyavahāra*, you will find you have that *śraddhā*. You will discover it. The beauty of anything done with *śraddhā* is just enchanting; it fascinating to yourself. Anyone who has *śraddhā*, a *śraddhāvān*, is admirable, but the *śraddhā* has to be in the right place, *śraddhayā aśraddhā tara.*

Finally, *satyena anṛtam tara. Anṛtam* is false perception. The world is not exactly as you see it; it is more than what you see. If so, what is the value in seeing? If you see that the world is more than what you see, and it is the truth, then your attitude towards yourself and towards the world will undergo a sea change. A change that makes you a person whose heart is so commodious that it can accommodate the world with all the people therein, with all their follies. You can accommodate all of them; you can accommodate your own guilt and hurt with a smile. That is the opening which we call 'opening up' of one's heart.

The Vedic view has got to be your view, if that is the truth. And the teaching is only to bring the Vedic view to your appreciation, to make you see as the Vedas see. To see yourself and the world as the Vedas see is such a blessing, and you are the inheritor of such a blessing.

Talk 3

Reality

We need to have certain minimum knowledge to live intelligently. We have no choice in making choices. And to make intelligent choices, our attitudes have to be proper. We do not acquire them naturally. Even if we acquire these attitudes, growing up in this Hindu society and culture, we need to understand them. An attitude without the backing of understanding is not well-founded; it can be swept away.

Life is now global. With all the TV channels available at our finger tips, we can bring any part of the world even to our car while travelling. So it becomes all the more important to know our culture that has been coming down the generations, why certain things are done the way it is done, and why we should know them; only then can we make an intelligent choice.

For instance, when we perform a *pūjā* at our home, we invite the priest. He asks for a spoonful of *haldi,* turmeric powder. With a little water he makes it into a lump, and says, '*asmin bimbe mahāgaṇapatim āvāhayāmi*—in this lump, I invoke Mahāgaṇapati.' This is common to our culture and we have been seeing it since our childhood. After all it is ordinary turmeric powder sitting in a container in the kitchen. We use it for making different dishes. It is not earmarked for this purpose. It is not separately ground and kept. But when we invoke Lord Gaṇeṣa in the lump of this powder, then every step of the *pūjā* we do is for Mahāgaṇapati. It has a direct connection to our view, the Vedic view, of everything being Īśvara. This is purely *bhāvanā*.

Vedic religion is rooted in knowledge and *bhāvanā*. This *bhāvanā* is not simply a kind of visualisation or contrived attitude. It is based upon a vision, the vision of what is, because all that is here is Īśvara. Any other concept of Īśvara which is other than this vision, the vision of the Veda, will be found wanting. It will not satisfy our reason, even the capacity to reason is undeveloped. Īśvara staying in a location is neither our vision nor our culture.

Without this vision, we cannot have all these *devatā*s, all the temples where there seem to be galleries of Gods, especially in the Hindu temples of North America. It is so because those who build these temples come from different parts of India. Naturally each one has his or her *iṣṭa-devatā* and wants that *devatā* in the temple, and so he or she contributes for that. In Washington D.C there is a Śiva-Viṣṇu temple in which we can see all the temples of South India. It looks as though we are worshipping forms, and therefore we are criticised by some people as idol worshippers. But we worship at an altar we are used to, without any prejudice to any other altar.

Our whole life is lived in forms because life is nothing but an expression of and dealing with forms. Whether we talk in English or in Tamil, in Greek or Latin, we are using a language which is nothing but forms. Every script is a form. Every pronounced letter is a sound form. Every word is a form. When we are looking into the meaning of a word like 'pot,' it reduces itself to a form. Any transaction is only through forms. In dynamic living, there is nothing but form. When I say, '*namaste*' it is a form, 'Hi' is a form, 'Bye' is a form. What is not a form? When I congratulate a person by garlanding or by shaking the person's hand, it is a form. All that is here are forms.

If God is formless, then what about all these forms? We ask the question, 'How did this form come about?' Then God comes into the conversation. A formless God, having a location, and very definitely male, is a concept that is full of problems. The Vedic view should be understood against the background of other contemporary theological concepts.

I am holding this pot in my hand. To make you understand Vedanta, I do not need any powerpoint program; all I require is this pot. Suppose I ask, "What is this?" Everyone will say, "It is a pot." But I say, "I do not see a pot!"

"Swamiji, what is wrong with you? It is a pot."

"No, I do not see a pot; I see only clay."

Please listen carefully. What I am holding in my hand is a pot according to you. But I see it as clay.

You say, "No, no, this is a pot."

I ask, "Do you not see the clay?"

"Yes, I see the clay."

"Then where is the pot?"

"The pot is on the clay?"

"What? The pot is on the clay? This flower is on the clay, because I can take it off. If the pot is on the clay, I should be able to take it off. Can you take the pot off the clay?"

"No, no, it is not on the clay, it is in the clay."

"In the clay? In the clay is only clay; there is no pot anywhere. If there is a pot, what is its weight? It must have some weight. The weight of your pot is the weight of the clay. So you have a weightless pot which is not sitting on the clay, which is not inside the clay. So where is the pot? There is no pot."

"Swamiji, you cannot say there is only clay. After all, the pot is there and you also know that the pot exists."

You have a *nāma*, a word, 'pot,' that has a form *rūpa*. The word 'pot' has meaning; it is a form which has some function. Mere clay cannot hold water, but clay in the form of pot can. It can also crack; then we say that it is a cracked pot, and a cracked pot cannot hold water. You can pour water into it, but it cannot hold it. Therefore, there is such a thing as a pot. This is magic, the magic of the *ṛṣis*. I hold in my hand what you call a pot, and I make it disappear! It is the Vedic vision, not an ordinary vision. You have a very rich tradition and you have to be ready for it.

You have words and words, tree, flower, leaf, root, fruit, bark, branch, twig. There are different words for different objects; all of them are words, nouns. Then you have words that are adjectives, big, tall, short, small, sweet, bitter, loud, feeble. And you have verbs, gone, comes, sits, sleeps. You understand these words.

You also need to cover an important aspect of the human experience. You have words like 'real' for which there is no object. It may be used as an adjective, but there is no object called 'real' that we now know. Let us use this word 'real' as a translation for *satya*. If a paper-flower is mistaken for a real flower, the perception has to be dismissed by the word false which is said as *asat* or *anṛta*

You need another reality word to cover human experience. Have you ever seen a square circle? You have seen a circle within a square; you can think of it. But what is a square circle? The word that is used for this is *tuccham*. Have you seen the flowing hair of a turtle? It is also *tuccham*. It does not exist. The word *tuccham* is used to refer an unholy compound, like a square circle or *vandhyā-putra*, the son born to a woman who never gave birth. There is no particular object for it.

We use the word '*satya*' which is not an object to convey our understanding of an object in terms of its reality. So too, the other two words, false and *tuccham*.

Everything in this world is considered *satya*. Sometimes, we do not look at *satya* as it is, but in our own way. Therefore, it becomes subjective. Projections are possible with an object becoming the locus for our projection. A person can be mistaken for another person. The person is real, but our perception is wrong. This is our problem, really.

There is another kind of mistake. We do not take one person to be another but we take the person as having certain attributes which the person does not have.

For instance, "He disappointed me."

"Why?"

"I thought he was a kind person."

"Now what has happened?"

"He is not kind at all."

"Why?"

"I asked him a small loan, and he refused. How can I say he is kind? He is not."

That person's understanding of kindness is wrong, and his understanding of this person as kind, in his view, is wrong. Therefore, the conclusion that he is not kind is also wrong.

This is how people are viewed, especially if they are closely related, and more so if the person is a spouse.

Adhyāsa is seeing something else in the place of what is, just as you see a snake while what is there is a rope. You need to have a word to indicate it is false. You also need a word to show in the falseness there can be an exaggerated value, such as thinking money is everything and dedicating your whole life to it. This is called *śobhanādhyāsa*. The opposite is *aśobhanādhyāsa,* because you are afraid of things that you need not be afraid of, like shadows.

It is clear, then, you need these reality words: *satya; asatya* or *anṛta,* which are interchangeable, and *tuccham*. These words do not have an object but they are words revealing your understanding of the world. It is very important because what you pursue is what is *satya* for you. Power is *satya,* in your vision, or money is *satya*. We can use the three words, *satya, anṛta, tuccha,* to understand the reality, and to reveal our understanding of the reality of an object. I will take them one by one.

The pot that you see here, is it *tuccham,* non-existent? No. So one word is gone. Then it may be false. Is it false? No. It is a real pot. If it is false it will not hold water—this one will hold certain volume of water, and if you pour in more, it will overflow. It means it is real, in keeping with a *niyati,* order. What about the clay? You cannot pour water into the clay (and retain it there) as you do it into the pot. But if you say pot is false, that statement will not hold any water! Therefore, what is pot? Two words *tuccha* and *anṛta* have gone now. What should the pot be? Every one concludes it is *satya*.

The Veda does not conclude that way. It has a vision to reveal. The Veda asks you a question. Can you see the pot without seeing the substance of which it is made? If the substance is clay, can you see pot without seeing clay?

What you are looking for is *satya*. But if you call pot as *satya*, what about the clay? The weight of your *satya*-pot is the weight of clay. The nature of your *satya*-pot is the nature of clay. The touch of the *satya*-pot is the touch of clay, it's brittleness etc., all belong to clay. Therefore, what object will you refer to by the word *satya*? Pot or clay? Before the pot was born it was clay. After the pot is gone, it is going to be clay. Even when the pot is there, there is clay.

You cannot dismiss the pot as non-existent, *tuccha,* nor as *anṛta,* false. You cannot take the pot as *satya* because *satya* is given to clay. Then what is pot? The word pot, its meaning, form and function, draws its being from clay here. When you say, 'the pot is,' it means 'the clay is.' The 'being' of pot belongs to clay. Yet there is a pot with form and function. This is what we call *sṛṣṭi, īśvara-sṛṣṭi*. Even though it is a human creation, the possibility of making a pot is all in *īśvara-sṛṣṭi.* A pot is a possibility. It is given. There is in your mind a particular meaning for the word pot. If an object fits the word meaning you have, you will call it a pot. So too for a jar, a lid or cup made of the same material or any other. Are there many clays, then?

There is only one clay. *Satya* is clay; the pot is in between. The pot is neither *satya* nor *asatya—sadasadbhyām anirvacanīyam*. That which cannot be stated categorically as *satya, tuccha*, or *asatya* is *anirvacanīyam*. It is only for want of a word that the human being is driven to pursue things that have no valid existence on their own.

There is only one *satya* and that happens to be you.

"Is this so?"

"Yes."

"Then am I *satya*?"

"Yes."

"Is my mother-in-law also *satya*?" (Laughter).

"I am sorry, yes."

When you understand this, you come to know that the whole *jagat*, including your body, mind, senses, is nothing but forms. All these are forms; words and their meanings. Once you understand this, the whole Vedic way of life comes alive.

Talk 4

Vedic View:
All that is here is all-knowledge Īśvara

Life is nothing but forms. When you deal with forms, you are also endowed with a form. Without form you cannot deal with forms. Endowed with a form you deal with forms.

We saw the word pot, like any other word, does not have a substantive. The chair on which you are sitting has no substantive. What you mean by chair consists of wood, cloth, some foam and many other words. The meaning of one word 'chair' contains many words, referring to many objects. If you take another word, 'cloth' for instance, it also contains many words with no substance of its own. 'Fabric' is a word; it has no substantive. When you look for some fabric, you end up seeing the yarn. When you look into the yarn, you find it is just a word called yarn; there is no substance, but only a form. Yarn is just fibres.

All the way you see only forms. Even time, past, present, future, is a form. You speak of the present using the present tense, but if you analyse the present tense, you will become tense, really. For instance, Ramu was cooking. At 10 o'clock in the morning I asked, 'What is Ramu doing?' The host said, 'Ramu is cooking.' At 11 o'clock, I asked him, 'What is

Ramu doing?' 'Ramu is cooking.' That time was the present and this time also is the present. What is the length of time for the concept of the present? You can say the current century is the present. Then the current year is the present, the current month, current week, current day, current hour of 60 minutes. Then the current minute and the current second which has one million micro-seconds, which in turn has one million pico-seconds, and so on. You can keep on dividing a unit of time.

So, the present is subject to infinite mathematical division. The present has no definite length of time but is subject to division into past, present, future; past, present, future; past, present, future. What is the present? Any one length of time is subject to further division, mathematically. So is there a time that is not subject to division? No. Any concept of time is time consciousness, no matter what its length. The content of time is consciousness, free from time; it is timeless.

The content of time is also the content of everything else in time, all of it being forms, as you will see. A year is a form, a month is a form, everything that you see, that you come across is a form. And the person who comes across all of it, is endowed with a form. You say, 'This is a body.' I would like to find out where the body is. 'Body' is a word, and for that word there should be some substance. If you say, 'It is the dermis,' that is the topic of a dermatologist. What is flesh? What is muscle? Again, they all consist of different cells.

Where is the body? It is just a bunch of cells. It is amazing. The body is porous, but you do not see that. If you look at the body with a microscope, you will never say, 'I love you.' (Laughter).

Please understand, this body is nothing but a form consisting of many forms, *nāmni nāmāni*; one name consisting of many names. It is all forms put together called *sṛṣṭi*. It is true all the way. Consider the senses, the eye, for instance. What is the eye? The eyelid is not the eye, muchless the pupil or the retina. Any one of them is not an eye, but put together in a certain way, they form an eye. Merely putting them together will also not make an eye either; it has to function. It has to be intelligently put together. Only then is it called *sṛṣṭi*. Form alone is *sṛṣṭi*.

Our *ṛṣis* knew what this *jagat* is all about; they knew it thoroughly. There is nothing to believe here. If there is something for you to believe, they make it very clear that it is a matter for *śraddhā*. Our *śāstra* talks of realities. But reality is something that can be talked about only when it is understood. It is not a matter for belief. You are not bound to beliefs. Somebody says one thing and others can refuse to believe it. It is the nature of belief. There is nothing to prove, and there is no necessity to prove anything; you just accept it for no reason. Thank the *ṛṣis*, you are saved from this kind of situation.

Your self-worth is exactly the worth that you have for your parents, your culture, religion, tradition and the wisdom that comes down the tradition. As as an individual you do not stand unconnected to your culture and religion, for the religious person is the core person. To be a Hindu you need to have this minimum knowledge. Unless you have self-worth, there is no self-acceptence. Self-respect is not to be gained by titles, qualifications, public acknowledgements or awards, but by owning up the self, the core person who remains untouched by these awards. Without knowing, without understanduing this vision, how can you have self-respect? Interference in a culture is so damaging. You must validate the child's heritage. In our AIM for Seva[5] homes, we validate the culture of the children who come from mountains and forest regions. They have their own dance forms, their own music. We ask them to dance and they feel validated. That validation makes them flourish, and will make them flourish.

Now, as I was saying, this physical body is a form that is intelligently put together. To explain a given gland, you have to use so many names, so many words, each of which has a form, a meaning. Words and their meanings are all that you have, all the way. What is being dealt with and the one who deals with it, are both words and their meanings.

You dream; it is given to you. That you can dream is a fact, and the faculty to dream is given to you which is another fact. You are the creator of the dream world. You think of the sun, and the sun is there in time and space.

Please note, you do not create time, you do not create space, you just think of sun, and along with sun comes space and time, *deśa* and *kāla*. This is what we hear in the *Dakṣiṇāmūrti-stotra, deśakālakalanā vaicittrya citrīkṛtam*...manifested as wonderful diversity along with space and time."[6] Modern physics also say that time and space come along with the manifestation. Think of the earth, of mountains, trees, rivers, birds, think of people, different people, all are there at once including a body for yourself. In dream you create the entire *jagat* and a body for yourself in the image of the person who is on the cot.

You create this *jagat* out of what? Out of your knowledge; it is all your knowledge. Your knowledge of sun in time and space, is the sun in time and space. It is your knowledge of mountains, that is the mountains; your knowledge of river, a river; your knowledge of trees, the trees, knowledge of birds, the birds; knowledge of cows, the cows, and your knowledge of people, the people in the dream. Every one of them is your knowledge.

Please understand, the whole dream creation, *sṛṣṭi,* is your knowledge. You are an individual, but you are Īśvara to all the people in the dream. You created all that is there in the dream. You pervade the dream; the subject and the object are you. Then you wake up, and everything resolves into you. The dreamer and the dreamt world too, resolves into the waker, and you say, 'It was my projection.'

Because you have the knowledge, you can think of it. Once you do, there it is. It is how the dream is; you think and therefore it exists.

The world is your valid perception of what is. Your body is not your projection. In order to project you need a body with a mind; both are given. They are available for common appreciation, in *vyavahāra*. This common appreciation is neither real nor subjective. It is neither false nor non-existent; it is inbetween. I can use the word '*mithyā*' for this reality.

This pot is *mithyā*. That which draws its being from something else is *mithyā*. Any form like pot has its being in the knowledge of what it is. When you understand this and look at the *jagat*, you understand it as forms which are the meanings of words. You can say it is your knowledge of what is, and it is all intelligently put together. What is intelligently put together presupposes knowledge. The whole thing is *jñānātmakam*, in the form of knowledge. There is nothing more than knowledge. It is the Vedic view, and it is supposed to be your view and vision. The Vedas are not meant for *ṛṣi*s. *Ṛṣi*s have given the vision of the Vedas to us, to humanity.

In the Vedic vision, the *jagat* being what it is, is purely knowledge—knowledge of Īśvara. He is the maker, and he is the material as well. To understand the Vedic vision we require to see these two causes in one. For instance, if there is a pot, there should be a pot-maker and there should be some material, clay. Only then can he make a pot. Without clay or some other substance, the pot maker cannot make a pot, unless he makes it out of himself. He has to find the clay in himself which will give rise to all kinds of problems! The point here is that the creator of any given thing is different from what the person creates, and also from the material he or she uses. The baker is different from the material of which he bakes the bread. It is true when we are talking of a bread or a pot, or any given thing of the same type in the *jagat*. But when the Veda talks of the entire *jagat* including space and time within the *jagat*, it is entirely different.

Time and space were considered absolutes in classical Newtonian physics, but not any longer. With quantum physics they have progressed merely to repeat, 'You are only saying what we are saying.' But we have been saying this for a long time. We have been saying for ages that space is part of the whole arrangement. We do not think of an object without space and time. The whole thing is intelligently put together. It is just vibrant, everything in motion; it is all one dance. It is what Naṭarāja is, just one being in motion.

The whole *jagat* is one conscious being, in motion. Look at the earth; it is moving, moving on its own axis, and then again, moving around the sun. The moon is going around the earth because it is born of earth. The earth being a planet, the moon is her satellite. Everything is moving, the whole universe is held in motion, by the grand force of gravitation.

Look at Naṭarāja. The *jaṭā,* matted hair, of Naṭarāja is horizontal showing the motion. The dance stops, it is *pralaya;* the dance starts, it is *sṛṣṭi,* it is a meaningful dance, because everything is meaningfully created. There is knowledge involved. Every movement, every *karaṇa*[7] has its own message to convey. What a marvellous vision. The whole thing is just a choreography of the all-knowledge Īśvara, the single dancer. We depict it as *devatā*s, Indra, Varuṇa, Agni, who are all different forms in the dance, a dance being nothing but different forms of expression of the dancer. Any one thing we see, it is the same dancer.

In the Vedic view there is nothing that is not Īśvara. Stars, planets, including the earth, trees, mountains, rivers—what is not Īśvara? Therefore, the material is not separate from the conscious being, all-knowledge Īśvara. Any knowledge, small or big, has to rest in a conscious being. Wherever there is knowledge, there is a conscious being.

You are a conscious being and you have knowledge. Even if you say, 'I do not know,' you know, at least, that you do not know. You are a conscious being with some knowledge; Īśvara is all-knowledge conscious being. Does all-knowledge Īśvara require a material to bring the *jagat* into being?

If there is a material separate from the conscious being, then that material should be somewhere in space and time. But the *jagat* is yet to come into being, space and time being part of *jagat* is also yet to come, like in sleep. Sleep is a great example to show how there is no space and time experience where there is no object, no world.

So, the material for *jagat* cannot be away from Īśvara because in *pralaya*, before *sṛṣṭi*, all that was there was Īśvara. "*Sad eva saumya idam agre āsīt ekamevādvitīyam*..., this entire *jagat* was, before, the one non-dual being."[8] The maker and material are one, the all-knowledge conscious, Īśvara.

When you look at everything, it is all given. The universe is given; possibilities are given. That new things can come up, and they come up, is also given. That you can put certain things together, hardware, software, it is all given. The faculties to put them together are given. So there is nothing that you can really create, nothing. You can only put together what is there, and from a standpoint, say, 'I have created this.' You can also destroy it and say, 'I have destroyed this.' You cannot destroy anything, really speaking. You cannot destroy matter, much less can you destroy energy. Everything is given. And this given can never be separate from the giver because what is given is the knowledge of the giver. It is all one knowledge that is here. Therefore, *īśāvāsyam idaṁ sarvam*.[9] You view this entire *jagat* as Īśvara, Naṭarāja in motion, without motion.

The man in the village who had never heard or studied the Veda, says, 'All that is here is Bhagavān.' It is *vṛddha-vyavahāra,* the Vedic view of life. The Vedic view is known not only by those who had access to the Veda, but also through *vṛddha-vyavahāra,* this knowledge has percolated to the last man in the hills. The whole Bhārat has this Vedic view by this age-old mode of communication, *vṛddha-vyavahāra.*

Talk 5

Being connected to the Infallible

The whole *jagat* is but name and form, *nāma-rūpa*. Every word and its meaning—whether it is a tree and its meaning, a leaf and its meaning, a flower and its meaning, stamen, pollen, any word and its meaning—in any discipline of knowledge, is intelligently put together and has its place in the scheme of things, serving a purpose. It means it is placed there intelligently. It is given. So, we are constrained to use the word creation.

The moment you use the word creation, the concept of a separate creator, different from the created object, is assumed. It seems obvious, but then, it is not true. For reasons that we have seen, the creation is non-separate from the creator, like in dream; the whole creation is the creator's knowledge. So too, the *upaniṣad* reveals, this *jagat* is created from a source who is all-knowledge and all-power; all that is here, known and unknown, he created, *idaṁ sarvam asṛjata*.

Further, the *upaniṣad* says, this creator became the whole thing, using one more verb, *abhavat*. *Asṛjata*, he created, *abhavat*, he became. *Satyaṁ ca anṛtaṁ ca satyam abhavat*.[10] It means, all that is here, with form and which is formless, that *satyam*, all-knowledge and all-power, became. It is astounding but that is what it is.

Modern quantum physics tells us that everything you see is nothing but quantum objects. There is nothing tangible. At the quantum level there is no object separate from your knowledge. It is an object of knowledge. Therefore, the entire *jagat* is a manifestation of the all-knowledge Īśvara.

This is the Vedic view, the view of what is. Unless we have this view, we cannot be objective because without the view of what is, we live in our own world, of our own making. We do not see the world that is for public appreciation, but look at it through our own goggles. Certain things become objects of our likes, and so our way of looking at them is entirely different. Certain other objects become objects of our dislike, and to certain objects we are indifferent, even if it is there it does not matter; we do not bother about its existence. So we do not look at things as they are. They are not just objects of knowledge, but objects conditioned by our own leanings, likes, dislikes and indifference. Therefore, we are not in the world of public gaze. We are not in harmony with **what is**.

The Vedic view is an important view, a non-negotiable view. There is no choice to be objective or not. You need to be objective. There are situations in life that are pleasant and not that pleasant. You have got to face them and respond to them. How are you going to do that?

The responsibility of a self-conscious individual, as I said in the beginning, is very great. To every situation you have to respond. Even if you say, 'It is not my responsibility, it is his or her responsibility,' that is your response. You have an unenviable situation of having to respond to all situations. Even if you need some help, and you get it, then you have to respond to the help. For some it is impossible to delegate work; it is also a response. The incapacity to delegate is a problem of needing to be in control. When you need to be in control, manipulation is inevitable.

You look at people differently and think that it is only you who can to do the task at hand. You have no time to do it either. Such people cannot accomplish anything in life because they have to be in control, and to be in control is to operate within a predictable area. It is a problem, and you need to know that you have this problem. Even if you have help, the fact remains that you need to respond. And there is only one person in your life to respond—you. Everything is a situation you face, and you have to respond to that situation.

If you are totally programmed, like a cow is, then you have no choice. You will be responding to every situation according to the programme. A human being is not programmed. But sometimes you behave as though you are. At other times you are very deliberate, and it is confusing. As a human being you are bound to be confusing until you take charge of yourself.

So, the Hindu way of life is in keeping with this Vedic view, that is, you have to be in harmony with **what is,** which is Īśvara. To be objective is to be in harmony with Īśvara. Without Īśvara, there is no objectivity; there is no pragmatism. It is the Hindu view of life for which you need to acknowledge the existence of the reality of **what is.** If **what is**, is missed, you cannot be pragmatic. To be pragmatic is to be objective, and to be objective is to acknowledge **what is**, and **what is**, is Īśvara. What choice do you have?

It becomes very clear when you look into your own responses. The first person singular referred to by the word, 'I,' is invariable. Being invariable, the person is always present, but not entirely in the same way. There is a small change according to the situation, a relevant change, which is centred on yourself. The person, as son, father, husband and so on, has to respond more often than not in terms of action. The *Bhagavad Gītā*, based upon the *veda-śāstra*, recognises it as *svakarma*.

What is *svakarma*? You can see here how the way of life is connected to the view. It has to be connected because you are a part of the whole. You are highly connected, no longer isolated.

yataḥ pravṛtirbhūtānāṁ yena sarvamidaṁ tatam
svakarmaṇā tam abhyarcya siddhiṁ vindati mānavaḥ
(*Bhagavad Gitā* 18.46)

Yataḥ, from which cause, from whom; *bhūtānāṁ*, the entire *jagat* consisting of elements and elementals; *pravṛttiḥ*, creation. *Yena sarvamidaṁ tatam*, by which it is sustained.

The one from whom this entire *jagat* has come into being in time and space, by whom it is sustained and pervaded, that Īśvara, revering whom, through *svakarma,* a human being gains success, *svakarmaṇā tam abhyarcya siddhiṁ vindati mānavaḥ.*

Svakarma is one's duty, what is called for at a given time and place, in a given situation. *Mānava* is a human being, someone for whom the mind is predominant. That human being gains success in life, *siddhiṁ vindati,* by being objective. We are going to look into this situation.

There is so much to say about objectivity. There are people who introduce themselves saying, "Swamiji, I am very pragmatic. I do not pray or go to temples, nor am I interested in all these talks on *Gītā* and so on. I am pragmatic." It is a very common expression. Do you mean to say only non-pragmatic people need these teachings?

Real pragmatism is to acknowledge the existence of **what is**. The reality of what you face, the reality of what others face, are both covered by Īśvara. Your body is a manifestation of Īśvara's knowledge, and it is given. Your *prāṇa,* your senses, your mind, all your faculties are given. What is given is not separate from the giver's knowledge, as I have already shown.

You need to assimilate the fact that this all-knowledge is manifest in the form of *jagat*. All that is here is either unmanifest knowledge or manifest knowledge, unmanifest knowledge before *sṛṣṭi*, and manifest knowledge after *sṛṣṭi*. Even in the manifest *jagat*, new things keep manifesting. It is not that after manifesting, Bhagavān went to sleep. He is *ananta-śayana*, lying down, but not sleeping. He has limitless power, *ananta-śakti*, symbolised by his lying on a snake. *Śakti* is likened to a snake, a slithering power because snake has no legs, but moves so fast. So *śayānaḥ sarvaṁ bibharti*, while in repose, he sustains everything; it means creation is not a one-time event. Within the created *jagat* there are new manifestations all the time. A new star can be born, an old star can burn itself out to become a black hole. A continuous process is going on. Within the created *jagat* there is further *sṛṣṭi*, further possibilities manifesting. This is how the *jagat* remains very dynamic. And *jagat* is not separate from Īśvara.

If this truth is assimilated, you will find your subjectivity at its minimum. You have to say it is the minimum because, in spite of security being your nature, it is security that you are seeking. Therefore to reduce your subjectivity, to be able to respond to every situation objectively, you need to recognise Īśvara who is all-knowledge. How do you assimilate 'all-knowledge' Īśvara? You recognise all-knowledge in terms of order. This is how I present Īśvara, so that you can assimilate Īśvara as all-knowledge. The whole thing is one whole, and we view this whole as so many orders.

There is a physical universe. We can, therefore, acknowledge one order, the physical order, which includes all the galaxies, constellations, systems like our own solar system, planets and satellites. On this planet there are different life forms, like plants and trees formed from a sprout which breaks out of the seed, *udbhijja*. Then there are the twice born; first comes the egg, and then what is born of the egg, *aṇḍaja*, like birds and reptiles. And we have *jarayuja*, those born from a womb, like mammals and so on. And finally *śvetaja*, like mosquitoes, lice including bacteria etc., which depend upon certain amount of moisture and so on for their birth. All these are here on this planet. The physical universe consisting of different things, including time-space, is what we study in physics, the physical order.

The life forms comprise the biological order. No life form is outside the biological order, and no system is outside the physical order. Īśvara, all-knowledge, is this physical order and this biological order. Once there is a life form, including a plant, it has a physiological system which implies a physiological order. Any physiological disorder is also within that order. In our tradition we have a beautiful means to assimilate Īśvara in the form of total physiological order, which is *prāṇā, sūtrātman*. Those who follow the tradition will say, while eating, *prāṇāya svāhā, apānāya svāhā, vyānāya svāhā, udānāya svāhā, samānāya svāhā, brahmaṇe svāhā*, meaning I offer (this food) to *prāṇa* and so on, which have different physiological functions within the body. The *prāṇa* is the individual *prāṇa*, the respiration and everything connected to it. Then, there is *apāna*, evacuation, which is done by the kidneys and so on; *vyāna*, circulation which implies the whole system consisting of heart, arteries, veins, capillaries, and all that is involved in circulation. Then *samāna* converts everything that is eaten to the same basic nutrients, *samīkaraṇakaraḥ*. It is the digestive system, liver, stomach, pancreas, everything that processes food.

The function of *udāna* is unique. The span of an individual's life is called *āyus*, and within that period, the *prārabdha karma* of an individual has to be exhausted. How is the span of life determined in this cosmic order? By an allotted number of breaths. You breathe in and breathe out, constituting one breath. With the completion of each breath, one of the allotted breaths is gone; the remaining longevity keeps decreasing. One clever man thought he could extend his life-span by stretching his breathing time; breathe in sloooowly, breathe out sloooowly, then do not immediately breathe in, just wait for a few seconds; it is called *bahiḥ-kumbhakam*. Then breathe in slowly, but do not immediately breathe out; this is called *antaḥ-kumbhakam*. Now suppose this man has been doing this and has stretched his life to another 15 years. A practical person is bound to ask him, 'What did you do in these 15 extra years?' 'I was breathing.'

Udāna is the time-clock that ticks away the life at the level of the individual, *vyaṣṭi*. The *vyaṣṭi* has to be a part of the total, the *samaṣṭi*. This is mentioned here in the sentence, *brahmaṇe svāhā*. Here Brahman means *sutrātman*, total physiological order.

There is no individual who is independent of the total. So you are highly connected. I had mentioned that the baby, before birth, is connected to its mother, *jananī;* it was safe, secure. The only time a human being is totally secure is when he or she is not yet born, formed alright, with an independent heart beating, but not yet born, connected to the creator. Once the child is born, the connection is gone and the child is isolated. Being too small to survive, the child is always in a panic. It goes to the flip side of the *ahaṅkāra* to form what we call the unconscious. It is within the psychological order of Īśvara.

The child's trust is total, and when the trust is total, the trusted person must be all-knowing, all-power, present all the time, totally consistent, should not fall ill, should not grow old, should not move away, should not change moods. But the reality is different. There is inconsistency that deeply confuses the child. Naturally, the unconscious gets loaded. It gets loaded and loaded and loaded for more than four years, and waits for marriage to take place. When one marries, there is a trusted person again, and everything will come out on that person. That person also has his or her own unconscious, and will project it on the spouse.

Thus the couple suffers not knowing what is happening and not knowing what can be done. It is all a projection from the unconscious. The person sees things that are not there now, but were there before when one was a child.

You need to get connected again, to the one who is infallible. Your whole life seems to be one of longing for the one who is infallible. Everybody is found wanting, everybody is fallible. So, you cannot put your whole heart and soul in one place. You keep looking for the infallible, and that infallible should be connected to you. That is what the presence of the infallible is; it has to be very much with you. In your awareness there should be no absence of the infallible.

The Vedic view of life makes sure that you have this, because it is already there. It is there in the form of physical order, of which you are a part, *vyaṣṭi*, being necessarily included in the total, *samaṣṭi*. You are sitting, not flying away or levitating, because of the physical order. Time, space, the sun and its energy, are all within the physical order. Every cell is pervaded by the biological order. You are pervaded. When are you away?

There is the presence of Īśvara in the form of physiological order, in hunger, thirst, and in disorder in the form of back pain and headache. Īśvara in the form of psychological order includes your unconscious. Psychology is your unconscious; otherwise you will only have beautiful emotions like love, compassion, sympathy, understanding, openness and so on. It is innate, spiritual, and a natural expression of yourself. Your own fullness manifests in that form. You call it emotion for want of another word, but really it is a manifestation, a dynamic form of the essential nature of yourself. Jealousy, hatred, fear, scheming—'what I can get out of this introduction,'—loneliness, all these fall within the psychological order.

Love and compassion are just you which is why when you express love, there is joy; you are harmless. People wait for you to be in a good mood. How can you predict when a person will be in a good mood? All moods are potential, unlike in grammar, waiting to surface from the unconscious. You have to accept that. It is Īśvara's order. Every whiff of an emotion is within the order of Īśvara. Therefore, in your loneliness Īśvara is present. In your unhappiness, in your pain, there is so much Īśvara. It is a very, very unmistakable presence. In pain you need not look for Īśvara. He is very much there in the form of your pain. Can you see that? That extra seeing is required, the change in the scales of your vision that lets you recognise the presence of Īśvara so clearly, that you can never be isolated from Īśvara. At what time will you be away from Īśvara? The *vyaṣṭi* is always pervaded by *samaṣṭi* in every situation.

In knowledge, the presence of Īśvara is very much there because every knowledge is Īśvara. That is the reason why you become happy whenever you understand something which was challenging like a puzzle. At that time there is nothing between you and Bhagavān in the form of knowledge. Memory also is Īśvara. It is a *śakti, medhāśakti. Medhā* is not just remembering alone; it includes your capacity to hold a topic for a length of time, enabling you to look at a topic from all sides. *Medhā* is given; in this there is Īśvara. In *apohana,* forgetting, also there is Īśvara, '*...mattaḥ smṛtirjñānamapohanañ ca,* from me is memory, knowledge and forgetting. [11]

Apohana is also suspension. What you know and can remember is not always in your mind, thank God! Otherwise you would never be able to have a new perception. That you can suspend everything you know is a blessing; it keeps you open to reshuffle your notions in the wake of new knowledge. Gaining right knowledge against a notion is possible only when the notion remains suspended, and your mind is kept open. What a capacity! It is how you have been learning. You have been re-editing your knowledge, reshuffling your ideas, looking at them from various angles, and seeing what is the truth. That capacity, *medhā-śakti,* is a given capacity which is a form of Īśvara. *Medhā* is Īśvara as even *apohana*. It is all one order, the order of knowing.

The all-knowledge Īśvara, in the form of one *mahā* order, whose presence is always with me, is infallible. I am now connected to the infallible, secure, safe, very safe. I accept my unconscious, I embrace it, welcome it, because it is all Īśvara. This awareness is not ordinary; it liberates. This is how I solve the sense of isolation from the whole. To be objective is to recognise this particular fact. Then, I am called upon to respond to various situations within this whole. How does that take place? It is the way of living.

Talk 6

Being in harmony with Īśvara

What is, is Īśvara who is addressed by different names, each name having a revealing meaning. Īśvara can also be invoked as a *devatā*. When you invoke a *devatā*, you are invoking Īśvara in a given aspect of Īśvara's manifestation. When you touch a wave, you are touching the ocean, but your *bhāvanā* is to touch a wave which is not separate from the ocean. You can touch the same wave and invoke the ocean.

You can invoke Īśvara as *vighna-hara*, the one who removes obstacles, and in the same *vighneśa*, you can invoke the total, Īśvara. In any one form you can invoke Īśvara, but any one form cannot be the total Īśvara because you look upon it as an object. Please understand, the whole vision of our Vedic view and way of life being what it is— everything is a manifestation of Īśvara. You invoke Īśvara, the total, in a single manifestation every day.

In the *Bhagavad Gītā*, Lord Kṛṣṇa mentions a few significant things for our discussion here. At one place he says, '*kāmo 'smi bharatarṣabha*, I am in the form of desire, Arjuna.'[12] Here, *bhūteṣu* means 'in the human beings,' because of an additional clause, '*dharma-aviruddha*, that does not transgress *dharma*.' A desire may not conform to *dharma*, for you do not have any control over that desire arising.

Desires occur and have their own causes, most of which are in the subconscious and unconscious. Because of this, certain desires may not be in keeping with *dharma*, but then you do not back them up. You do not attempt to fulfil any one of them and they remain fancies.

To fulfil a desire, you plan and take action and you make sure that what you do is in keeping with *dharma*. This is the Vedic view and way of life. Desire also is the Lord, is the Vedic view of life. The action to fulfil it without transgressing *dharma*, is the Vedic way of life. Lord Kṛṣṇa tells us in this sentence, '*dharma-aviruddho bhūteṣu kāmo 'smi, dharma* is I; *kāma* is also I.' That a desire occurs in your head is within the order of Īśvara. Besides the conscious, the unconscious and the subconscious are given. If you have viewed some things with certain attitudes, they become the causes for desires to occur later. How do you buy into ideas? Depending upon that, you pick up the causes for your desires. There is nothing wrong with it, for it is within the order of Īśvara. The Lord does not say, you should not have desires; it would be wrong to say that. Nobody can be expected not to have desires. Such a statement from a book like the *Gītā*, for which you have so much *śraddhā*, would drive you crazy. You would have permanent guilt about having desires. The reality is, you have no say over them.

With respect to action, you have a choice, *karmaṇi eva adhikāraḥ te.*[13] Once done, the result is taken care of, inasmuch as the action and its result are connected; it is given. If you clap your hands, the result will be there. You clap your hands and cannot request your hands not to make any sound. If that is the result you want, you have to bring your hands together differently, as you do in *namaste*. Therefore, literally you have freedom in your hands. Well, you are free, you have a choice in your action, *karmaṇyeva adhikāraḥ te*.

Bhagavān says, 'I am in the form of any desire in your head.' Therefore, let there be more Bhagavān! Do not complain, 'Swamiji, I have so many desires.' Let them be there. But when you fulfil those desires, make sure that your actions do not go against what is universally accepted as an ethical value structure, the norms that everyone has to conform to.

You are endowed with choice. I am equally endowed with choice. Both of us must have a common basis to exercise our choice. This basis is universal, only then will every human being know it without being taught. Nobody can plead ignorance of *dharma*. You can plead ignorance of a man-made law, because a new law can be enacted at any time by the ruling party of our country. But nobody can be ignorant of this universal value structure. If someone did not have the knowledge of a matrix of values that is common to all, it would be a lacuna in the very *sṛṣṭi*, in the manifestation of Īśvara. We are talking of the all-knowledge which is Īśvara; there is no question of any defect there.

The *jagat* is well done;[14] there is nothing deficient in *sṛṣṭi*. Only our knowledge is deficient.

Now, ask people a few questions like, 'Do you want to get hurt?' Ask anyone; each one of them will answer the same, 'No.' Ask them, 'Do you want to be robbed? 'No.' Do you want to be cheated? 'No.' 'Do you want your land to be encroached upon?' 'No.' Encroachment, in our Vedic view, is a very big crime, attracting capital punishment, which is why we did not occupy others' land; we did not colonise. One becomes an *ātatāyin* when one takes away someone's property, *kṣetrāpaharaṇa* and the punishment is death.

Dharma is universal. Everybody expects the truth from others, and the expectation from others is the same. Everybody expects that all others should be compassionate, sympathetic, understanding, giving. It is common, which is why it is called *sāmānya-dharma*.

The *sāmānya-dharma* is universally appreciated by people, without being taught. It is picked up by common sense; it is innate. Even animals do not want to get hurt, but they do not know that you do not want to get hurt. If they sense danger to their lives, they will attack. The cow will not have any guilt when it gores somebody to death because it does not know that the person does not want to get killed. It only knows that it does not want to get hurt. So it is always right.

I, however, know both. I know what others should and should not do to me, and I also know others expect the same thing from me. It means I know exactly what do you want from me, and, of course, what I want from you is also very clear to me. Since we both know that, it is the same for both of us, it is given and it is universal. When it is so, it should be like knowledge of a tangible thing. Knowledge is always of an object. Here too, there must be an object for us to know.

The verb 'know' being transitive, has an object. I know. What do you know? I know *dharma*. It is an object that I know. But it is not an external object, it is embedded in the cognitive person, and it is available for me when I have to make choices. Therefore *dharma* is in the minds of human beings and *dharma* is protected only when the *dharmin* is protected. If *vaidika-dharma* has to be protected, the one who upholds *vaidika-dharma*, the *vaidika-dharmin*, has to be protected.

All over the world there are people who uphold *dharma*, without even being religious. You do not need religion for this, because *dharma* is given. Appreciation of *dharma* as a manifestation of Īśvara makes you a person who is in touch with Īśvara, in harmony with Īśvara. It makes you totally objective.

Desire and *dharma* are both manifestations of Īśvara and therefore, to fulfil a desire you cannot go against *dharma*.

But then, the problem is, desires have power. They release a lot of pressure, *vega*. When a desire remains unfulfilled, the *vega* born of desire, and born of anger later, drives you to go against *dharma*. *Dharma* is Īśvara, so you cannot go against it. Desire also is Īśvara, but you cannot hurt yourself in fulfilling the desire by going against *dharma*. When you fulfil your desires in keeping with *dharma*, you are in harmony with Īśvara. Bhagavān is only talking about his *vibhūti*s when he points out he is the desire that is unopposed to *dharma*. That a human mind can desire is one of his *vibhūti*s. And that the human mind has the knowledge of universal *dharma*, *sāmānya-dharma*, is also Bhagavān's *vibhūti*. Both are *vibhūti*s, and you cannot afford to go against the other.

Living is dynamic; you acquire new desires as you keep living. But *dharma* remains the same. The i-Pod was not there before, nor was the laptop; which is why previously some empty laps were always available for the children. Now no lap is empty because of the laptop. Well, new desires will come, but our good old *dharma* will ever remain.

Dharma, Hindu *dharma*, being universal, we can talk about it to anyone, anywhere. We are not talking about a belief system which will come into conflict with another belief system here or elsewhere. When we assimilate the two *vibhūti*s of Īśvara, *kāma* and *dharma*, we do not succumb to the pressure of desire. The *Gītā* says this in its own words:

indriyasya indriyasyārthe rāgadveṣau vyavasthitau,
tayorna vaśam āgacchet tau hyasya paripanthinau.[15]

*Rāga-dveṣa*s are desires. 'I want to have this and I want to retain this' are both *rāga*. I want to have a job, I want to have a house, I want to have this experience, I want to go there, I want to create this, I want to make a name for myself, all these are desires, *rāga*. I want to avoid something or someone, such as it should not happen to me or I want to get rid of something. These are the opposites of *raga*; they are *dveṣa*s.

Wanting to gain, to retain, and wanting to avoid, to get rid of, creates a lot of pressure when you do not have space within. Whereas, if there is leisure within, satisfaction centred on yourself, you can manage all these likes and dislikes. There is inner leisure that allows you to conform to *dharma*. Desires become simple *vibhūti*s only when you do not transgress *dharma*.

It is only in the Vedic tradition that *dharma* is an end in itself, a *puruṣārtha*. The end never justifies the means. The means itself is an end for us, because *dharma* is Īśvara for us, which is why Lord Rāma is worshipped as an embodiment of *dharma, rāmo vigrahavān dharmaḥ*. We look at him as Īśvara standing as *dharma* with two hands and two legs and call him *nīla-megha-śyāmala-varṇaḥ*; this is Rāma, *dharma*. Consequently the Hindu way of life is non-aggressive because *dharma* is the means and it is the end as well, *puruṣārtha*.

I have to explain *puruṣārtha* here. *Puruṣārtha* is that which is sought after by all human beings, *sarvaiḥ puruṣaiḥ arthyate iti puruṣārthaḥ*. Who does not want security? Who does not want money? Who does not want real estate? Who does not want name, power, etc.? All these are *artha*, and everybody wants them. Then people want satisfaction, pleasure, simple sensuous pleasure or aesthetic joy. These are all different avenues of satisfaction, *kāma*, that people seek. *Artha* and *kāma* are common to all.

Just as wealth, satisfaction, pleasure and so on are ends, so too, *dharma* is an end in itself, *puruṣārtha*. In fact, it is the first *puruṣārtha* because you need to be in charge of yourself. To be in charge of yourself is to be in harmony with *dharma* which is Īśvara. Since desire also is Īśvara, you cannot go against *dharma* in order to fulfil a desire. But desires, being what they are, will drive you to cut corners. Therefore, you need to know how to say, 'No'. This is where you require *satsaṅg*, your daily prayer, *nitya-karma*. All these are important because they help you gather strength. You ask for help and you have a support system; you are not helpless. The will can become weak for many reasons which is also within the psychological order. Your enemies may or may not be outside, but they are certainly inside. You work towards *dharma* and that is success. Do your *svakarma* which is in conformity to the universal ethical norms.

You know *dharma* as simple ethical norms, but what you need to know is a little more. You should be able to interpret *dharma* in a given situation. *Hiṁsāṁ na kuryāt*, never cause any harm to anybody. Yet a surgeon cuts open the abdomen, removes the tumour, and in the process the patient dies. The surgeon is paid. Someone else does use a knife to attack a person and he pays for it. Similarly a teacher may cause a kind of hurt to his or her student when he has to point out the fallacy of some ideas and notions which would prevent proper understanding. A wrong notion held for a long time with emotional commitment is bound to hurt when pointed out as wrong by the teacher. In both, helping is the motive, not hurting.

Dharma is so very dynamic that you find in the epic like *Mahābhārata*, people seemingly or wrongly interpreting situations. Where they are supposed to do certain things, they do not do them; conventions become very important. Dharmaputra himself said that he did not want to play dice. However, there was a convention that a king or prince should accept an invitation from a person of equal status for a game of dice. Duryodhana quoted this particular convention; Dharmaputra succumbed to that. Instead, Dharmaputra should have said, 'No. I am not interested in gambling even though there is a convention.' That is all he had to say and all these problems would not have been there; there would also be no *Mahābhārata* war. It points out that even a great person is subject to some wrong leanings. Convention is a big thing, but you do not need a convention in which you can lose your shirt, and

Dharmaputra lost it. You learn from the *Mahābhārata* that *dharma* is very dynamic.

Let us see the verses that follow:

"...*svadharme nidhanaṁ śreyaḥ paradharmo bhayāvahaḥ*, it is better to die doing one's own duty..." [16]

The 18th chapter of the *Bhagavad Gitā*[17] again mentions one's duty as a means for spiritual success.

What is *svakarma*? There is no particular action called *svakarma*. *Svakarma* is what you are supposed to do daily and on certain occasions. *Karma* is *kārya*, what is to be done in a given situation. The Veda has a vision, and it does not want you to under-achieve. You are highly connected. Only when you establish that connection, can you claim the wholeness that is you, that is yours by nature. It is the step which we will see in the next talk.

Here, the concern is with neutralising your likes and dislikes. It is neither possible nor necessary for you to get rid of your likes and dislikes. You need to remove their power of making you transgress *dharma*. It is your aim, your culture of 'duty'. Our understanding of duty has kept us going. There are people everywhere who have an understanding of duty, but in our culture it has got to be there. Your duty, *svakarma*, is the thing to be done not only at this time, at this place, but in other places and times as well.

Ahiṁsā, not-hurting, is a *dharma*, while *hiṁsā*, causing harm is *adharma*. And there are different shades, different ways of *hiṁsā*. You can do *hiṁsā* even by disregarding etiquette. You can have a doubt in a given situation not only about a course of action, but also about your own conduct. *Vṛtta* means conduct. Conduct that is purely etiquette is also important. Every sphere has its own etiquette, even tennis. Every culture has its own etiquette. A western dinner has its own protocol and you need to follow, if you do not want to disturb the people around. It is living a life of least disturbance. Even in this *dharma, ahiṁsā* is involved because of your commitment to a life of least distrubance. So you need to know where you are, what is the situation, and what is proper here. If you do not know,[18] there are people who know what is proper and what is improper. Talk to such persons who are committed to *dharma*.

Your presence should be such that it does not disturb anybody, but is welcomed wherever you go, in any situation. It is possible, for this is our culture. I quoted the Veda here only to prove that this is the Vedic view and way of life. Our ways of living are based on the view.

There are people who think that those who do not believe in their religion are enemies to God. Therefore they can be killed, and the ones who kill will go to paradise. This implies the end justifies the means. We cannot hurt Īśvara for Īśvara's sake. Our *dharma* is universal; we do not need religion to tell us what *dharma* is. But religion should confirm *dharma*, as we do, and has something more to say that is equivalent to *puṇya* and *pāpa*.

TALK 7

Svakarma is Īśvara

Dharma is a *puruṣārtha*. You then need to employ your will and initiate a process of growth so that you conform to *dharma* without any conflict while playing different roles in life.

Another important fact in our vision is we play different roles. Each role has a script which undergoes changes relevant to a given situation. So you need to see what is your script now. It is a very important element in deciding your duty, *sva-karma*. Unless you have space between the person and role, they become one and same. Understanding life as role-playing is not seen in any other culture. Shakespeare had a sense of it, as any great mind would, but whether he did see through the whole thing we do not know. He said,

> "All the world's a stage,
> And all the men and women merely players;
> They have their exits and their entrances;
> And one man in his time plays many parts.[19]

Definitely he had felt, men and women are but players, because one is called upon to play roles every day.

The 'I' is invariable, the roles are variable. That you are a son or daughter is a basic role. Then you have roles like brother or sister, wife or husband, father or mother. You do not have a choice whether to go by the script or go against it, for you cannot avoid role playing. A child is born, and you are a father or a mother. What choice do you have now? Wherever you go you have a neighbour. So, neighbour is a role, citizen is a role, employer is a role, employee is a role, and there is no role without problems.

How do you determine that they are roles? Our *śāstra* says, you are a *puruṣa* and everything that you do has got to be a role. You are a son when you talk to your mother or father; there is a mother's son and a father's son. The next moment you are talking to your grandfather, and you are a grandson. How much time does it take for you to shift from being a son to a grandson? No time. Then again, think of your brother, and you are a brother; just think of your brother, that is enough. Then you think of your sister, you are a brother again with a shade different, of course. Think of your wife, you are a husband. Think of Bhagavān, you are a devotee. Then think of your children, and you are a father or mother. It means there is only one person.

I am the father, I am the mother, I am the brother, I am the sister, I am the spouse, I am the son, I am the daughter, the grandson, the granddaughter, I am the employee, the employer; these are all roles. This is *vyaṣṭi*, individual, a very dynamic role. It keeps changing, never static. But the basic person is the same, invariable.

Life is meant to be lived. Somebody asked me this question, 'What is the goal of life?' It is a very general question that gets different answers from different people. I answer, 'The goal of life is to live.' Death is not the goal of life. You are born and you must live. You can ask, 'What does it take to live my life?' My answer is, 'You need to be alive to **what is.**' Otherwise it is just living the life of a somnambulist, dream walker, living in your own world, a world of your own apprehensions, projections, likes and dislikes, and getting carried away by them. That is not living. The Veda says, these are simple projections. You are supposed to reduce these projections to become more real and alive to **what is.** This is living.

One thing is inevitable, and that is relating. Life is relating. You cannot avoid relating. I am not talking of relationships, I am talking of relating. You need to relate, then relationships and so on come later. You need to relate to the world. When you open your eyes, you relate. You first relate to your eyes; you open your eyes. If there is a connection between your eyes and the object that you see, you relate to, you have to respond to it. Either you are indifferent to it, or you dislike it, or you are afraid of it, or you love the object and want it. Relating implies response. Now, these objects to which you relate always change, whereas the I, that relates, does not undergo any change, being invariably present.

Dvau hi padārthau, there are only two things, one is I, the other is everything else. The teaching begins with *dṛg-dṛśya,* seer-seen; subject-object. When these two are there, subject and object, I am invariably present in every role I play. Even though I am invariable, to some extent I undergo a small change. To my parents, I am a son or daughter, to my siblings, I am a brother or sister. This change centred on 'I,' has to be relevant to what I relate to.

So what is relevance? The relevance is the script that I am supposed to follow. For instance, in a play, the actor 'A' assumes the role of 'B' a begging person. But after the play, he does not go out on the street and start begging. For the play, he plays the role of a begging person and even studies the nuances of beggary. In fact, he knows he is going to be richer by being a beggar for sometime and therefore begs like no real life person who begs can beg. The script calls for him to bring tears from his eyes, and he does brings those tears, congratulating himself thinking, 'I am crying so well!'

That is the space between the role and the person. It has nothing to do with physical space and nothing to do with time. The difference between the two is not brought about by time. It is not that the role is now, and later the person will come. No, that is loss of self-identity. There is no space-time, *deśa-kāla,* division because the role is the person; the role stands where the person stands.

The role's body is the person's body, the role's thought is the person's thought. But then, would not the person also be the role? No. Why do they not roll into one? The role's problems are confined to the role. They do not have any power to affect the person—not the person behind the role, but the person; the role is the person. These expressions like 'the person behind the role,' 'at the bottom of the role,' 'the substratum of the role,' are all wrong; they mislead people. The role is the person. Then why is he not affected? Because the person is not the role.

B is A, A is not B. In your initial algebra lessons you learn that *b* is *a*, and *a* is *b*, but it is not so here. B is A, but A need not be B. A is always A. A is A playing the role of a son, A is A playing the role of a brother, A is A playing the role of a husband, A is A playing the role of an employer, an employee, a neighbour; all the roles are A, while A is not any of them; A is free from all of them. To whom is this basic person 'A' related?

A tree is standing in a forest. The next tree is a mother tree, and this tree is a child tree, a small one, coming up. Then there are sibling trees and neighbour trees. Some of them are alien trees planted around. So this individual tree is related to all of them differently, and it has different roles to play, as a neighbour tree, a daughter tree and so on. But it is related to the forest basically, as every other tree, without any change. Once the word 'individual' is used, the 'total' has already come to embrace the individual. I need not even say that. In *vyaṣṭi* the *samaṣṭi* is there, not away from the *vyaṣṭi* but pervading the *vyaṣṭi*. Everything is a manifestation of Īśvara whom you understand as all-knowledge. It is all-knowledge that is manifest here.

You assimilate the all-knowledge Īśvara in terms of physical order, biological order, physiological order, psychological order, and epistemological order (the order by which you gain knowledge). Then there is the order of *dharma,* whose other side is the order of *karma*. If there is no *dharma*, there is no *karma*. All the orders form the total sustaining you, the individual. You are more than connected.

Not only you are related to the total, your father is also related to the total; it is the same. Not a whiff of difference is there between your father as individual-total, your mother as individual-total, your child as individual-total, your grandfather, and great grandfather. It is the same, individual-total. This relationship is the invariable relationship.

In a relationship if there is something absolute, this is it, the individual-total. It is the only relationship that does not undergo any change whatsoever, no matter who is relating to the total, Īśvara. That person, related to Īśvara, is a *bhakta,* a devotee. This understanding makes your life objective; it allows you to play your roles appropriately and follow the scripts, without being affected.

Just a shift in your understanding; you are a devotee, basically. When you understand, *svakarma* becomes *arcanā*, worship. Whatever you need to do, it is your script; you have no choice. Just think about it. Think about the appropriateness of your response in a given situation. What is an appropriate response in a given situation? Is it something in your hands? Is there a choice? There is no choice. Even simple laundry I am including here; what choice do you have? If you have to do the laundry, you have to do it.

It is purely Bhagavān in the form of appropriateness, as the action that is to be done. *Kāryam iti yat karma,* the action that has got to be done, about which there is no choice; it is how Bhagavān is. The entire life of *vyavahāra* is Bhagavān. This is what the Vedic vision is; this is the idea of duty, *svakarma.* Whatever is appropriate, even sending a prompt e-mail, is *svakarma*. But it must be appropriate, not wasteful, like calling frequently just because you have a mobile phone. You may be able to afford it, but it is wrong to spend money listlessly—money is Lakṣmī. You respect her. Even if it is offered free, your redundant call would add up to the net affecting someone's urgent call.

To be a *vaidika* means to be a person who is exposed to the reality of living. We need to be objective, which means we need to be in touch with Īśvara. All that is here is Īśvara, who does not come only once a week. Everything is Īśvara.

Our problem is the profundity of our tradition. It is not a simple doctrine or set of beliefs for which our thinking has to take leave, never to come back. It is profound, the appropriate action to be done at this time is Īśvara and it is *svakarma*.

Svakarmaṇā tam abhyarcya siddhiṁ vindati mānavaḥ. You play different roles with different scripts appropriate to a given situation. The script is ***svakarma***, duty. Our society is duty based. The duty of the parents is the right of the children and the duty of the children is the right of the parents. The duty of the husband is the right of his wife and the duty of wife becomes the right of her husband. Then, the next question will be, 'What are the husband's duties, Swamiji?' Well, his duty is to make his wife happy; her duty is to make him happy.' You have to learn that. Whenever there is a merger, you must learn, you have to yield. In America there are freeways which have no traffic lights or intersections. When another road joins it, there is an access ramp approaching the freeway from an angle. Slowly it joins and at the point where there is a merger, there will be a sign saying 'Yield'. Because there is merging of traffic, the traffic on the freeway has to yield to the merging traffic.

What is marriage? It is a merger. Then yield! You have to yield to make the other person happy. It is not one-sided, 'I am the husband.' So what? You are lucky to play the role of a husband. Somebody chose you, and you have your duties. Duties are never one-sided. The concept of one-sided duties is wrong and creates so many family problems.

In your daily duties you are also alive to the *devatās*. You do not take the sun for granted. You do not take the air for granted, or the water, your *pitṛ*s, or the *ṛṣi*s. You do not take any of them for granted; you remember them and pay your dues to them. It is the Hindu way of living, the Vedic way of living, because you are connected to all of them. Since you are benefitting from them, *svakarma* includes your obligations to all of them. It is all one *yajña*. The entire life becomes a *yajña*; it is the *vaidika*'s life. You are basically a devotee. And that involves doing your *svakarma*. Otherwise, it is like one branch of a tamarind tree saying, 'I do not like being part of a tamarind tree. I want to be part of a mango tree.' It is madness. You have to enjoy what you are enjoined to do.

You are basically a *bhakta*. It is the *bhakta* who plays all roles. First you are a *bhakta*, last you are a *bhakta*. In the middle, of course, you are a *bhakta* playing different roles.

When this is the situation you can assume a few more roles. You can become a *sevak* of AIM for Seva. One more role, one that makes a difference to society. For you, as a *bhakta*, it is a wonder that you are untouched playing all these roles. Untouched, unaffected, you lend joy to everything.

An example very often used to illustrate this is the lotus leaf. The water on the lotus leaf does not wet the leaf, not one bit. Not only that, the lotus leaf lends a glow to the water on it. The droplets shine like pearls while the lotus leaf itself is untouched by the water.

This is how your life should be. Basically you are a devotee who is unaffected by the numerous problems that every role has. You confine the problems to the role, you remain unaffected. It is true, but more than that, you lend a glow to all that you do with the freedom that you enjoy.

When there is freedom while playing a role, you are a role model for every one. Your awareness that you are basically related to Īśvara gives you the space to enjoy being a son/ daughter, husband/wife, father/mother. In fact, you are a devotee son/daughter, a devotee father/son and so on. The devotee is free from being affected. So, I leave you as a devotee.

Oṁ tat sat

NOTES

[1] Anaikatti is a small village on the Kerala-Tamilnadu border, near Coimbatore.

[2] *Bhagavad Gītā* 4.39

[3] A suburb to the South of Chennai.

[4] *Kolam* is a Tamil word for rangoli, a decorative design composed of curved loops, drawn at the entrance to the home around a grid pattern of dots, using rice powder. This is part of a daily ritual of caring for the fauna, called *bhūta-yajña*.

[5] AIM (All India Movement) for Seva is a nationwide movement initiated by the author, and has touched the lives of over 10 million people and children across 15+ States for integrated community development with a special focus on the needs of rural and tribal children.

[6] *Dakṣiṇāmūrti-Stotram*- Verse 2.

[7] A unit of dance.

[8] *Chāndogyopaniṣad* 6.2.1

[9] *Īśāvāsyopaniṣad* 1.1

[10] *Taittirīyopaniṣad* 2.6.1

[11] *Bhagavad Gitā* 15.15

12 *Bhagavad Gitā* 7.11

13 *karmaṇyevādhikāraste mā phaleṣu kadācana mā karmaphalaheturbhūrmā te saṅgo'stvakarmaṇi.*

(*Bhagavad Gītā* 2. 47)

14 *yad vai tad sukṛtam,* (*Tattirīyopaniṣad* 2.7.1

15 (*Bhagavad Gītā* 3.34)

16 (*Bhagavad Gitā* 3.35).

17 *yataḥ pravṛttirbhūtānāṁ yena sarvam idaṁ tatam,*

svakarmaṇā tam abhyarcya siddhiṁ vindati mānavaḥ

Through one's duty, worshipping him from whom is the creation of the human beings, by whom all this is pervaded, a human being gains success. (18.46).

18 *atha yadi te karmavicikitsā vā vṛttavicikitsā vā syāt. ye tatra brāhmaṇāssammarśiṇaḥ. yuktāyuktāḥ. alūkṣā dharmakāmāssyuḥ. yathā te tatra varteran...* (*Tattirīyopaniṣad* 1.11. 3 and 4)

19 As You Like It

Books by Swami Dayananda Saraswati

Public Talk Series :

1. Living Intelligently
2. Successful Living
3. Need for Cognitive Change
4. Discovering Love
5. Value of Values
6. Vedic View and Way of Life

Upaniṣad Series :

7. Muṇḍakopaniṣad
8. Kenopaniṣad

Text Translation Series :

9. Śrīmad Bhagavad Gītā

   (Text with roman transliteration and English translation)

10. Śrī Rudram

    (Text in Sanskrit with transliteration, word-to-wordand verse meaning along with an elaborate commentary in English)

Stotra Series :

11. Dipārādhanā
12. Prayer Guide

    (With explanations of several Mantras, Stotras, Kirtans and Religious Festivals)

Moments with Oneself Series :

13. Freedom from Helplessness
14. Living versus Getting On
15. Insights
16. Action and Reaction
17. Fundamental Problem
18. Problem is You, Solution is You
19. Purpose of Prayer
20. Vedanta 24x7
21. Freedom
22. Crisis Management
23. Surrender and Freedom
24. The Need for Personal Reorganisation
25. Freedom in Relationship
26. Stress-free Living
27. Om Namo Bhagavate Vāsudevāya
28. Yoga of Objectivity

Bhagavad Gītā Series :

29. Bhagavad Gītā Home Study Program (Hardbound) *

Meditation Series :

30. Morning Meditation Prayers

* Under print in new format

Essays :

31. Do all Religions have the same goal?
32. Conversion is Violence
33. Gurupūrṇimā
34. Dānam
35. Japa
36. Can We?
37. Moments with Krishna

38. **Teaching Tradition of Advaita Vedanta**

Exploring Vedanta Series : (*vākyavicāra*)

39. śraddhā bhakti dhyāna yogād avaihi ātmānaṁ ced vijānīyāt

Books by Pujya Swamiji's disciples :

Sadhvi Varadaa Caitanya

40. Bhagavad Gītā Home Study Program

    (Hardbound) Kannada translation based on the original Gītā Home Study Program—English.3 Volumes available.

Dr. Carol Whitfield

41. The Jungian Myth and Advaita Vedanta
42. The Vedantic Self and the Jungian Psyche

Books by Smt. Sheela Balaji :

43. Salutations to Rudra
    (based on the exposition of Śrī Rudram by Swami Dayananda Saraswati)
44. Without a Second

Also available at :

ARSHA VIDYA RESEARCH
AND PUBLICATION TRUST
32/4 Sir Desika Road
Mylapore Chennai 600 004
Telefax : 044 - 2499 7131
Email : avrandpc@gmail.com

ARSHA VIDYA GURUKULAM
Anaikatti P.O.
Coimbatore 641 108
Ph : 0422 - 2657001
Fax : 0422 - 2657002
Email : office@arshavidya.in

ARSHA VIDYA GURUKULAM
P.O.Box 1059. Pennsylvania
PA 18353, USA.
Ph : 001-570-992-2339
Email : avp@epix.net

SWAMI DAYANANDA ASHRAM
Purani Jhadi, P.B. No. 30
Rishikesh, Uttaranchal 249 201
Telefax : 0135-2430769
Email : ashrambookstore@yahoo.com

AND IN ALL THE LEADING BOOK STORES, INDIA